SELECTED POEMS

First published in 2008 by
The Dedalus Press
13 Moyclare Road
Baldoyle
Dublin 13
Ireland

www.dedaluspress.com

ISBN 978 1 904556 78 7 (paper)
ISBN 978 1 904556 794 (bound)

Dedalus Press titles are represented in North America by Syracuse University Press, Inc., 621 Skytop Road, Suite 110, Syracuse, New York 13244, and in the UK by Central Books, 99 Wallis Road, London E9 5LN.

Printed and bound in the UK by Lightning Source, 6 Precedent Drive, Rooksley, Milton Keynes MK13 8PR, UK.

Typesetting by Beth Romano
Cover design: Pat Boran
Photo of John Jordan © Hugh McFadden

The Dedalus Press receives financial assistance from An Chomhairle Ealaíon / The Arts Council, Ireland

Selected Poems

John Jordan

Edited
with an Introduction
by
Hugh McFadden

ACKNOWLEDGEMENTS

Acknowledgements are due to the Editors of the literary magazines in which some of these poems first appeared; also to Michael Smith, of New Writers Press; to Peter Fallon, of the Gallery Press; and to John F. Deane, of the Dedalus Press.

To John Jordan's
'peoples'

Contents

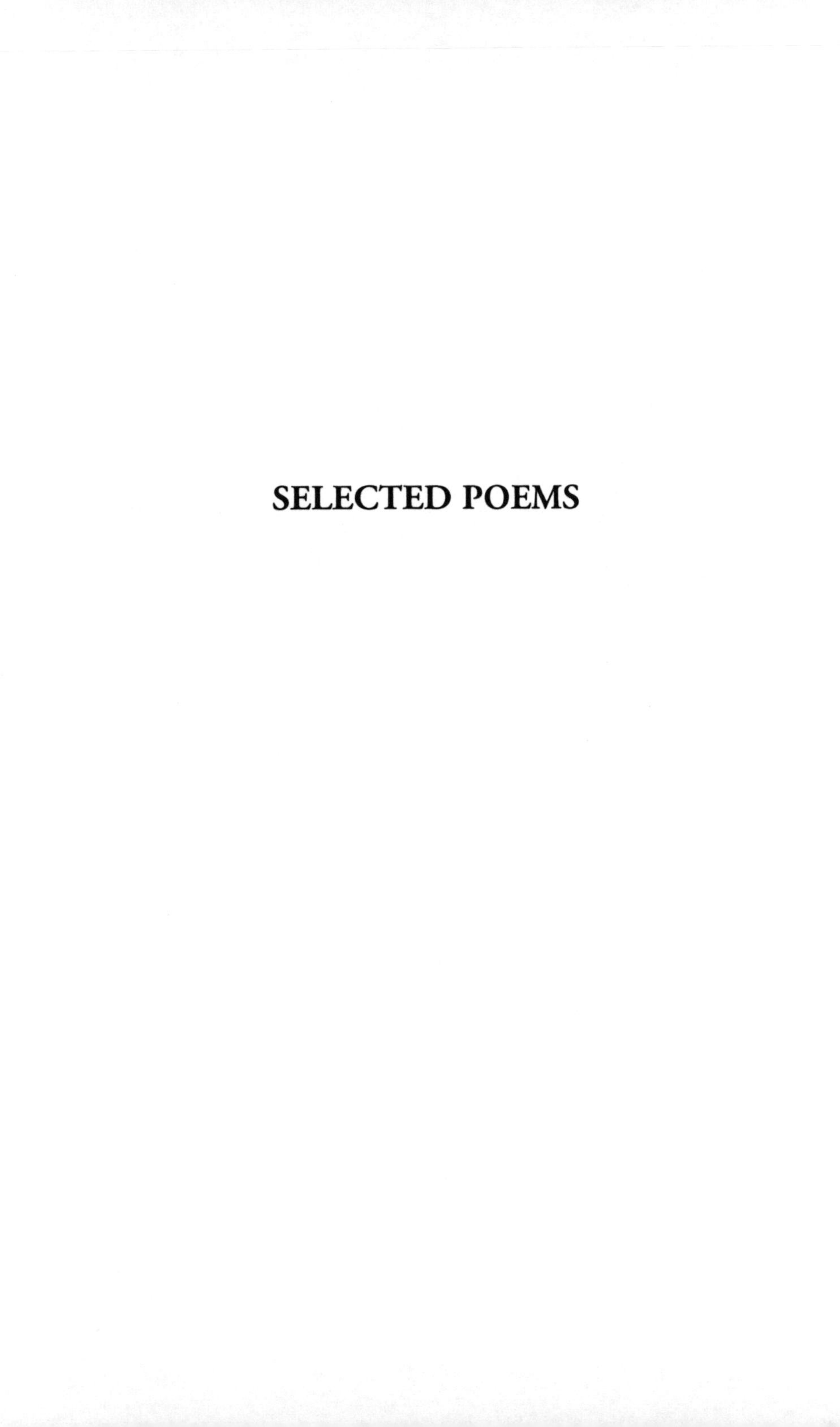

SELECTED POEMS

Introduction

As this Introduction is being written, in the Spring of 2007, the University College Dublin authorities are preparing to complete the college's final removal to Belfield of sections of the departments of medicine and biosystems engineering that until now had remained at U.C.D.'s buildings in Earlsfort Terrace. The college is preparing to mount in May an exhibition of memorabilia in Newman House entitled *Farewell to the Terrace,* and to publish a book of the same name. So it is fitting to remember here, in the preface to a selection of his verses, that the poet John Jordan was one of the most talented lecturers to grace the halls of learning in 'The Terrace' during the 1950s and 1960s, when he held teaching positions in the Department of English at U.C.D.

It was in the Physics Theatre in Earlsfort Terrace at the beginning of the Michaelmas term in 1962 that the present writer first encountered John Jordan, who was delivering—no, performing—a lecture on Chaucer, if memory serves me well. Present on that occasion were a number of students and friends of Mr Jordan who were to distinguish themselves later as notable poets and writers. Included in this number were: Paul Durcan, Michael Hartnett (then Harnett), James Liddy, Brian Lynch, Michael Smith and Macdara Woods. When he concluded his lecture, John Jordan invited me to join some of this company for a drink in a pub then called O'Dwyer's in Lower Leeson Street. So began a spiritual friendship that was to last until John Jordan's untimely death at the age of 58 in Cardiff, on 6th June 1988.

By the time this *Selected Poems* appears, 20 years will have elapsed since that death saddened his many friends in Dublin and removed from the literary scene one of the most singular and seminal influences in the development of poetry and literary criticism in recent times in this country.

There used to be a literary school of thought, once dubbed the *new criticism,* that poetry should be read (and *closely* read, at that) without undue recourse to biographical information about the author and his life experience. The text's the thing, we were told... the text, and nothing but the text. More recently some of our more prurient dons have begun to demand an *explanation* of the life of the writer, not just an *explication de texte.* Perhaps the noxious tendrils of the tabloidisation of our culture have reached even into the inner groves of *akadēmeia* and have begun to envelop the rarefied thoughts of the collegiate custodians of high art and literature... an Ivy Day in the Staff Common Room, as it were.

So, while adjuring 'our rostrum explicators' in their pedagogy to remember the use to which Louis Pierre Althusser put such concepts as Sigmund Freud's *Overdetermination*, here, briefly and crisply, is an outline of some of the more pertinent points of information about the life.

John Edward Jordan (1930-88) was born in The Rotunda Hospital in Dublin on April 8th, 1930, the elder son and eldest child of John Anthony Jordan and his wife Mary Agnes (*née*) Byrne. His father worked at the Guinness Brewery in St. James's Gate, Dublin: his mother was born in Jarrow, England, of Irish parents. The family, which included his sister Kathleen (Sr. Grace, of the St. Louis Order) and his brother James, lived in Park View Avenue, Harold's Cross, Dublin.

He was educated at Donore Avenue C.B.S. and at Synge Street, C.B.S., off the South Circular Road, Dublin, before gaining a scholarship to University College, Dublin. His teachers at the Secondary School in Synge Street included the novelist and broadcaster Francis MacManus: and his school-friends included the actor and broadcaster Ronnie Walsh (who later was the producer of the RTÉ Radio programme *Sunday Miscellany*, on which John Jordan frequently broadcasted); the artist Patrick Swift, and the poet Pearse Hutchinson, to whom several of these poems were dedicated.

While still at school he had developed his interest in literature and drama to such an advanced level that James Agate, the celebrated English drama critic who wrote for *The Sunday Times* and broadcast for the BBC, was astonished by the precocity of the young

Dublin schoolboy who began to correspond with him (*q.v.* 'Letters to Leo Pavia and James Agate', in *Crystal Clear: The Selected Prose of John Jordan,* Lilliput Press, 2006). From this correspondence it is apparent that the teenage prodigy had already read much of the great literature in English.

Through Agate's intervention with Hilton Edwards, John Jordan became an assistant stage manager at the Gate Theatre in Dublin, and in his mid-teens was reading drama scripts for that theatre's two directors, Edwards and MacLiammóir. For a number of years he acted at the Gate, most notably in that company's touring production of *Hamlet* at Kronborg Castle near Elsinore, Denmark. When he gained an Entrance Scholarship to U.C.D. he faced the dilemma of choosing either a career as an actor, or of pursuing his academic interests. He chose the latter, although he retained a keen interest in the theatre, and acted in university theatre in Dublin and later in Oxford.

At U.C.D. he took a Double First in English and French for his B.A. degree, and won the Laforcade Medal and Cup after a nation-wide contest in French in 1951, *concours oratoire et littéraire* (the runner-up was the poet John Montague). In 1952 he was awarded an N.U.I Travelling Studentship, the university's most prestigious scholarship, and shortly afterwards he became a Scholar at Pembroke College, Oxford, where he chaired the Arts Committee, was elected President of the Samuel Johnson Society, acted with the OUDS, and had some of his verse published in the university's literary magazine, *Trio.* In 1955 he took a degree for a thesis on English verse-epistles, 1590-1640.

John Jordan returned to Dublin from Oxford in 1955 and was appointed an Assistant in the English Department in U.C.D. He became an Assistant Lecturer in 1959, and College Lecturer in 1964. This writer remembers how good he was as a lecturer, recalls the extraordinary intensity with which he recited lines from Shakespeare's *Richard III,* on the miniature stage of the Physics Theatre in Earlsfort Terrace; how he brought Chaucer's *Canterbury Tales* to life, and gave really memorable lectures such as the one on

Johnson's 'On the Death of Dr. Robert Levet'. There was a good deal of the actor's art in these performances, married with the acute sensibility of an exceptional critic and close reader of texts.

In 1962 he began editing *Poetry Ireland*, that seminal 'Sixties magazine that continues to influence contemporary Irish poetry, in a line that proceeds through other such magazines; from James Liddy's *Arena* (co-edited with the late Michael Hartnett), to *The Lace Curtain*, *Cyphers* and the current successor to *P.I.*, *Poetry Ireland Review*, the first eight issues of which John Jordan edited in the 1980s. It is no exaggeration to suggest that had John Jordan not created the magazine *Poetry Ireland* out of the ashes of the 'Fifties journal *Irish Writing*, which had contained a supplement called *Poetry Ireland*, then the world of literary magazines in Dublin might not have developed as it did from the 'Sixties to the present time: in particular, *Poetry Ireland* itself as a society, and the *Poetry Ireland Review*, might not have come into being at all… which in no way is to diminish the work of those who assisted him in setting up the *Poetry Ireland* magazine in 1962, and those other editors who carried on editing *Poetry Ireland Review* after John Jordan bedded down the first eight issues and handed over the editorial reins to Thomas McCarthy in 1983.

By the beginning of the 1960s John Jordan had already established a reputation as an astute literary critic and a fine drama critic. As early as 1955, in *University Review* he wrote an incisive essay on Sean O'Casey, 'A World in Chassis', challenging the received idea of O'Casey as the 'Dublin labourer of genius' who wrote three great plays for the Abbey but went astray when he left for exile in England after the unfortunate *contretemps* with W.B. Yeats over the rejection by the Abbey Board (in fact by Yeats) of *The Silver Tassie*. The essay took apart this cosy thesis. At the age of 26, shortly after he had taken up a lecturing post at U.C.D., he reviewed Hugh Kenner's book *Dublin's Joyce* [q.v.], once again in *University Review*, and Richard Ellman's monumental biography, *James Joyce* (see, 'Joyce: One of the Boys', in *Crystal Clear: The Selected Prose of John Jordan* (Dublin, 2006).

Jordan chided those of his countrymen who had a supercilious attitude towards the Joyce scholarship being carried out by foreign writers, especially Americans. Indeed, the atmosphere in which he worked as a critic and an academic in Dublin at this time was stolidly conservative, socially and politically very cautious, even among some Establishment elements a little reactionary. In this *milieu* that was so 'safe' and middle-class, the essentially radical free spirit that was John Jordan attempted to carve out a body of critical work in journals and magazines that took in the best of Modernist writing, from Pound and Eliot to Joyce and D.H. Lawrence. He made the case for O'Casey and Synge as major playwrights in world literature, and examined the work and tragic legend of Oscar Wilde, when it was anything but safe to dwell very long on Wilde.

It was not an easy task in Dublin to be a critic with a popular audience and a high profile. In a 'Report on Thomas Kinsella' (q.v., *Crystal Clear*) John Jordan wrote: "If what follows has any value, it will be due partly to the fact that my judgments are not likely to be slavered by personal affection or dislike, by awe or envy. Dublin's literary jungle is probably no better or worse ultimately than that of any other city. The aggravating hazard, however, lies in the fact that the jungle is miniature and the beasts keep on running into each other."

In 'Off the Barricade' [q.v.], in *The Dolmen Miscellany*, he wrote: "Only in Dublin perhaps, is it necessary to announce that there can be such a thing as criticism unloaded with personal animus. But Dublin … is so ingrown in its literary alliances that the little verse-reviewing which is done is often pocked with timidity, and non-committal. There is, indeed, in the whole Irish literary world, a tendency towards the formation of Protection Societies. I too have lived in Arcadia".

The years from the mid-Sixties to the end of that decade were difficult ones for John Jordan, as a succession of friends died during that time. In 1964, Gainor Crist (whom J.P. Donleavy caricatured as Sebastian Dangerfield in *The Ginger Man)* died suddenly while on a sea voyage to the Canary Islands, allegedly after going on a drinking 'spree' with the captain of the boat. In March of that year, Brendan Behan died after he collapsed in the street, his final illness brought on by diabetes aggravated by his alcoholism. He was only one month into his 41st year. On 6th May 1966 John Jordan's friend Robert Mac Bryde, the artist, who shared a house in Upper Leeson Street with Patrick Kavanagh and others, was knocked down by a car and killed not far from the house. That same year, Flann O'Brien died of cancer in Dublin.

John Jordan, too, had experienced health problems. A bout of tuberculosis in 1962 had left his constitution very fragile. On holiday from his post in U.C.D he took ill early in the New Year of 1964 while on a visit to Gainor Crist and Pamela O'Malley in Barcelona (see, 'Haemorrhage', in *Crystal Clear*). By 1966, his life in Dublin seemed to have closed in on him: perhaps the strain of lecturing, writing, reviewing and much 'socialising' with his friends in McDaid's and other establishments had begun to take its toll. He got leave of absence from his staff post at U.C.D. and took up a position as Associate Professor of English at the Memorial University of Newfoundland, near St. John's, Canada.

While lecturing at the Memorial University late the following year, he heard the news of the death in Dublin of Patrick Kavanagh. It profoundly affected him (see, 'Obituary for Patrick Kavanagh,' and 'To Kill a Mockingbird', in *Crystal Clear).* Resigning from his professorship in St. John's he returned to Dublin to mourn his close friend. His health declined, and in 1969 he resigned his post at U.C.D. in what he called 'an amicable settlement', in order to concentrate his energies on creative writing and freelance literary journalism.

The 1970s produced a flurry of books in a few years. He had been hospitalised in 1969, not long after a trip to North Africa at the end of 1968. Out of this stay at St. Patrick's in Dublin came the startling poems in *Patrician Stations* (New Writers Press, 1971). The volume was dedicated to Austin Clarke, whose very fine long poem 'Mnemosyne Lay in Dust' it echoed, particularly in the verse 'A Guest of the Dean's'. *Patrician Stations* was praised by the critics, but later some commentators expressed regret that Jordan's earlier poems had not been collected and published first. In 1975 Gallery Press did publish early work (including the brilliant 'Second Letter to Patrick Swift'), together with later verses, in *A Raft from Flotsam.* In 1976 Gallery issued *Blood and Stations*, which contained two prose pieces, including 'The Haemorrhage', along with an expanded *Patrician Stations.* (For a discussion of Jordan's complex publishing history and how it may have affected his career, see Macdara Woods' Introduction to *The Collected Poems* (Dedalus Press, 1991), which was edited by the present writer).

In 1980, a limited edition of new verse, entitled *With Whom Did I Share the Crystal*, appeared. Its short poems are acute aperçus: they include antic pieces (e.g., 'For Julius Henry Marx') and elegantly restrained elegies for Kate O'Brien and Micheál Mac Liammóir.

By the mid-Eighties his physical health had begun to decline. He had had several bouts of illness over the years, exacerbated by his 'lifestyle' – he was a heavy smoker of un-tipped cigarettes and he had developed a growing dependence on alcohol. In 1986 he suffered a relatively mild stroke and was hospitalised briefly in Dr. Steeven's Hospital in Dublin. He made a recovery and went back to work. Remarkably, he retained an acute critical faculty.

At the beginning of June 1988 he went to Cardiff to attend the Cumann Merriman Summer School, which had gone on location there. He died suddenly in his hotel in Cardiff on the morning of 6th June, 1988. He was only 58. His burial took place in Mount Jerome Cemetery near Harold's Cross Green, not far from his home in Park View Avenue, after Requiem Mass concelebrated by F.X. Martin, O.S.A., in the parish church. His friends and fellow writers Ben Kiely and Francis Stuart delivered tributes in the church. Other writer friends—Paul Durcan, Pearse Hutchinson, Macdara Woods and the present editor—read poems at the graveside in honour of his memory. The late theatre director/actor Jim Fitzgerald recited lines from Shakespeare's Cymbeline: *Fear no more the heat o' the sun/Nor the furious winter's rages...*

2

The poems selected here are drawn from four books published in John Jordan's lifetime, along with a few other verses that were found among his papers. The four slim volumes in question are: *Patrician Stations* (New Writers Press, 1971); *A Raft from Flotsam* (Gallery Press, 1975); *Blood and Stations* (Gallery, 1976); and *With Whom Did I Share the Crystal* (St. Beuno's Hand-Printed Limited Edition, Mornington, Co. Meath). The sequence in which the poems appear in this *Selected Poems* follows the chronological order of the posthumous *Collected Poems* (Dedalus Press, 1991), with some minor changes regarding the positioning of the verse 'A Paella for Drivellers' and a few of the poems from the collection *With Whom Did I Share the Crystal.*

Like Caesar's Gaul, the poetry of John Jordan can be divided into three parts: the poems before *Patrician Stations* (1971), the poems in that collection so-named, and the verses collected in *With Whom Did I Share the Crystal,* written mostly in the 1970s. (There are a few others written in the 80s.)

As already indicated, the manner and sequence in which John Jordan's poetry was published was unusual, in that most of his early work was collected and published in book form after the publication of verse that was written much later. Many of the poems that made up his second collection, *A Raft from Flotsam,* were written in the late 1940s and in the 1950s, from 'Pub Poem of the '40s', to 'Entre Chat et Loup'. And there were several other uncollected poems also from the '50s, such as 'Self Portrait: Oxford' *(1958).*

A number of these early poems are particularly good and are astonishingly sophisticated for so young a writer: John Jordan was only 18 when he wrote the remarkable poem 'Second Letter: To Patrick Swift'. Sophisticated not alone in form, but in the attitude to the nature of the heart-breaking sentiments that are expressed:

While you were ranting your lyceum lines
careering the vaults of your glittering dooms,
bleeding at the heart from paper knives—
I have my nuances and Chekhovian glooms—
But we were both mummers and so we got on.

Mine was a mime of lime-scent and heart-break
quiet, frail, imbecile, thirsty for applause—
and O you knew that and nurtured me, because—
Thespis's children stick together
in sunlight and shower and weather
when the proud rose must surely fall,
thrown on a dump with all the rest of the trappings …

Other notable early poems include: 'Notes for an Obscene Sequence' ("The silver fox, my darling, /Will gobble up your breast, /O strip yourself, come quick with me, /Be naked, that's the test."); also the poem, 'Wordsworth Was Right' ("O to get out of it/ O to get out of it/ O to get out of it/ Or drink the Shannon dry!"); and, 'A Seduction of the '40s' ("There was a balcony too and they looked down into the garden / And he said, 'You know, darling, / Your breasts, I mean bosom, is like apples'. / She said: 'Don't give me that crap'. / They'd both seen Bogey in *Casablanca.*")

A poem written in London in 1951, 'An Old Letter', expresses a sense of deep *ennui*, at a time when the poet was just past his thirtieth birthday:

To begin with and in a manner of speaking
We live in the trenches.
You are on leave in the sunlight …
I want you to know how we wake
To the stench of tears, bloody sweat,
Eyes, heels, sore from the narrow patrols,
Lips smarted from incautionary kisses.

Already, a certain feeling of existentialist *angst* is apparent in his poetry: it was to deepen in later work and intensified in the verses written after a hospitalisation in Dublin, the poems that formed the collection *Patrician Stations.*

The anguish in the poems of the 40s and 50s was personal, temperamental: but John Jordan was also conscious of the general sense of malaise that pervaded post-war Europe. He grappled with the question of religious faith at a time when Europe, shocked by the horrors of the Second World War, had lost all sense of eternal certainties. He had visited London only a few years after the war ended, and he had seen the destruction wrought on the city and its inhabitants by the blitz.

Over the next decade or so he travelled in Europe and took the temperature, as it were, of the citizens of the Continent. Some of the poems from the 60s and 70s come close to expressing a sense of *weltschmerz* (universal sorrow), verses such as: 'Non Dicam' ("The mines are flooded, Christ, / It's dark again. /I must build a raft from flotsam…"); the verses, 'Gerard Dead 1 & 2'; the startling poem, 'Tidings From Breda'*;* as well as 'Excoriations on Mont-Seny …'

But the most heart-rending verses of all are those in *Patrician Stations:* poems such as 'A Guest of the Dean's', 'The Feast of St. Justin', 'Letter to Paul', and 'Heimweh'; along with the related poem, 'A Paella for Drivellers', which was written shortly after the others in the collection. These are poems of pity and terror, and are truly haunting reflections on the nature of suffering, the mystery at the heart of forgiveness, and the question of redemption. Out of a spell of illness that was very actual and real—not at all metaphorical—came some of the most moving verses of that troubled age. The lines echo Austin Clarke and Dean Jonathan Swift:

Great Dean, invigilator of our loves and liberties,
Here is United Ireland. The burrs of thirty-two counties
Stick in my heart. That cool twelve thou' has
Bought me fraternity. We are all experts here:

Schizophrenics, depressives, alcoholics, pathics,
Some elated like the Blessed Saints, others
Withdrawn into who knows what red hell or
Candid heaven, all are duly-elected members,
Academicians who may never resign, signatories
Of the treatment.
                    Woe to the formulators of empty oaths.
They may know again the quality of shipwreck…
                    …Madness is no laughing
Matter. Though some here laugh like madmen.

The verse 'A Paella For Drivellers', which really belongs with the *Patrician Stations* poems, is truly shocking in its vituperation against 'the lowest type of Irishman, the begrudger', and in particular the poet Robert Graves, for the latter's vindictive attack on Ezra Pound, whose *Cantos*, writes Jordan, are: "Our glory, our blotched marvellous glory". The poem continues:

For my heroes are people I fear to fight for:
Jews, Sephardic and Ashkenazy,
Palestine refugees, disloyal Kurds,
The world's great galaxy of Nansens,
God's chosen miserable …

The verse in its ferocity is somewhat reminiscent of lines in Jonathan Swift's epitaph, with its *saeva indignatio.* It is unique among Jordan's verses for this vituperation, and contains little or none of his often self-effacing humour.

But there is humour and not a little wit in the poems in his final small collection, *With Whom Did I Share the Crystal* (1980). A number of them are antic in spirit, particularly the marvellous 'For Julius Henry Marx (1891-1977)', and 'To Ms Mae West On Her 85th'.

Among the blazing azaleas
Of the Parque del Campo Grande
I perceived the true, sophisticated
Marxist point of view:
Let the people have duck soup;
Let them at the races lose their shirts,
Let them shirtless storm the Opera,
And stop the shrieks of Mimi with Coronas.
Chiefly, let them raise intemperate eyebrows
To the infinite spaces of the stars.

(For Julius Henry Marx (1891-1977)

This was written in 1977, on one of his many visits to his beloved Spain, in this case to Madrid and Valladolid. The poems written at this time also include notable elegies for his friends Kate O'Brien (who shared his love of Spain, particularly Avila), Micheál MacLiammóir, and the poet W.H. Auden. The verse 'Micheál', written in the summer of 1978 in Málaga, ends:

In a sub-tropical garden
Drenched in moonlight
Moths, midges, white butterflies,
Die on my cheeks,
As I cry for you.

His output declined in the 80s. Several of the 80s poems are sombre, particularly 'St. Pius Ward' (written after an experience in a Galway hospital), and 'The Short Unhappy Exile of Don Geraldo', with which this selection ends. This final poem in the collection concerns the Irish writer Gerald Brenan, at the age of 90, being brought from his home in Alhaurin el Grande, Málaga in May, to an old people's home in Pinner, Middlesex; and then being brought back to his house in Spain a month or so later, to die:

I wished to die, but yes, I wished to die,
till they said I'd drive them mad,
but not in a clean and well-lit place,
exiled from my things,
from my black tobacco,
from my roses,
from the street
Carlos Gross had them name for me,
poor Carlos whom I've survived ...

It is my hope that this *Selected Poems*, coming after the interest in John Jordan's work evoked by the publication of *Crystal Clear: the Selected Prose*, will re-establish his reputation at least in Irish poetry circles, as a writer of intelligent, stylish verses, the best of which are among the most interesting poems published here in his time, from the late 1940s to the early 80s. A number of these poems are truly memorable and should be included in anthologies of Irish poetry.

John Jordan was not fortunate in the manner of the publication of his poetry in his lifetime. The delay in publishing his prodigious early verse told against his hopes of establishing a strong reputation as a poet. He was probably better known as a literary critic while he lived. The variety of his talents as a literary critic, drama critic, academic, columnist, broadcaster and short story writer, took the focus away from his undoubted abilities as a poet. And the droll aphorism of Mark Twain may be apposite in his case: "Fortune knocks at every man's door once in a life, but in a good many cases the man is in a neighboring saloon and does not hear her"

To recap what I wrote in the Preface to the *Collected Poems*: This volume needs no further comment from me—except to paraphrase Ezra Pound's 'Note for T.S.E.', on the death of Eliot. His was a true voice—not honoured enough, and deserving of more than we ever gave him. Here, I will not write any more of my friend John Jordan, but will urge you: read him.

Hugh McFadden
Dublin, April, 2007

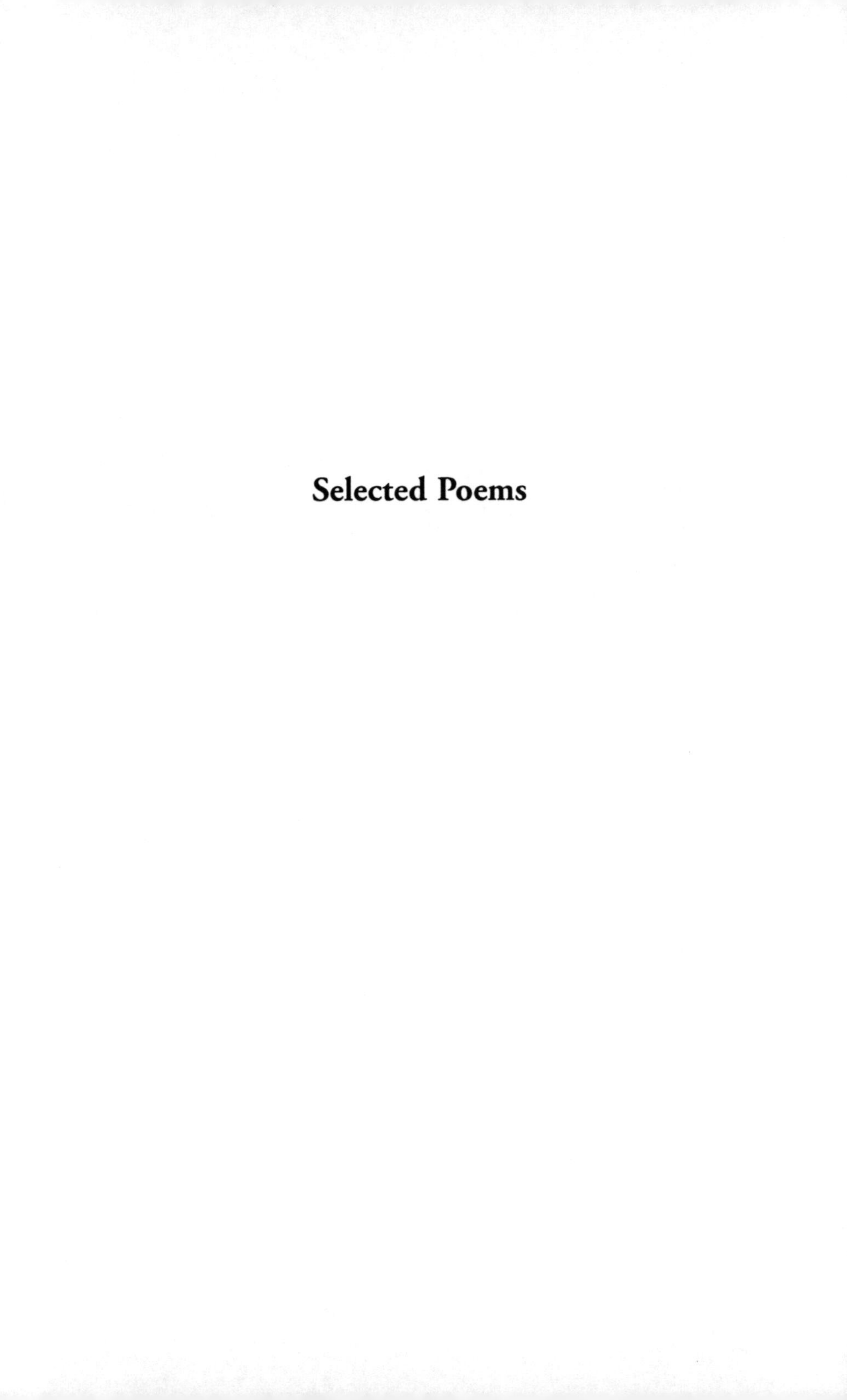

Selected Poems

Two Loves: 1

Her hair was burnished,
her eyes sombre with puzzlement,
her voice a sad birdy twitter.
The puppets ringed about the pond:
and, God, the pain of finite words,
the rounded agony of footling speech.

[1947]

Katie

For Katie the candle-glitter and the pine are worth the frost
At Mass-time in the Winter.
The household lie till nine until sausages and scramble,
When already she has knelt and clacked
A thousand Aves—Mary's marvellous currency
Of worn sweet words—
Earliest of payments for Katie's feather-bed
When the candles sputter out in the lambent night.
Bread of angels for breakfast when she goes home
Back beyond the womb and the scalding light.

[1948-49]

On a Friend in Love

They'll not forgive him,
Because he has not learnt the cosy tricks,
Like faked horse-sense,
That lure the comfortable, the advising, the middle-aged.

They'll never understand
That even in the oddest places,
Sootherin' Filda in the Abbey Bar
Stretched in Baggot Street—nothing can mar
His vision of the many-peaked star
That shines for men of art.

Part of what he tells us is utter nonsense
Part of what he tells us he does not mean
Part of what he tells us, tells to the perceptive
Why his eyes are like the sea and green.

But still we fear
That the too frequent tear,
And the hopeless thrall of a Yankee flapper,
May blast the vision, darken the eyes,
Pack off art with sophistry and lies,
And we shall raise a keen in the Abbey Bar
For the single-mindedness nothing could mar,
'O he broke his teeth on a hard old stone
He loved like a pearl of the sea'.

All join in and raise your glasses
'Gainst golden lads bound to brazen lasses,
'O he broke his teeth on a hard old stone
He loved like a pearl of the sea'.

[1948]

Notes for an Obscene Sequence

The silver fox, my darling,
Will gobble up your breast,
O strip yourself, come quick with me,
Be naked, that's the test.

Our trees of iron are just as fine
As shoots of flowering shrubs,
The martinis of my kisses
As good as gin in pubs.

You'll soon forget the pleasure trips
To Mayo or Shanghai,
But in the end you'll always feel
My hand upon your thigh.

So throw away the chicken legs,
Come fasten on my mouth,
And when you're glutted there, my bird,
We'll take a trip down South.

[1948]

Pub Poem of the '40s

1

'Come, come, come!'
Cry the Men of God,
And why in God's name don't I go?
But other mummers die
And the doxies they cry,
There are more things in life
Than brass tacks and a wife.

'Come, *do* come!'
Cry the Painted Men,
But why in God's name don't I go?
For me that mummer died,
For me his mother cried:
There are worse sides to death
Than rouge and baited breath.

The solution might be
To make a pass
At a decent, healthy,
Catholic lass,
With desirable paps
And intriguing thighs
And imbecility in her eyes.

To settle down (but where?)
Outside the town's the thing
And you'll always sing
If you're early to bed
And late to rise—and

What a simply smashing surprise,
When on a cold dark winter's night
She coyly whispers that the prize
Of strictly modest copulation
Is a Blessed Event—ah, what elation!
For we shall have done our duty!
And as everyone knows
(Including that priest with the mottled nose,
That charming thing who gave me a rose,
The boy who at Seapoint was chary,
The Scouts and Gampdom of Sairey)
Duty is beauty!

2

But rarely, perhaps, to go alone,
Alone on days with mist
When the glass moon comes early
And unseen gulls skim phantom
Barks that bear across the darkish water

My dear unreasonable courtesans.
Their milk is gamey
Smacking of fried fish and future pain.
They travel far with easy hearts,
And forget with whom they've lain.

Into the train!
Home to the daughter of J.J. Quinn
Home to the love that's free from sin,
And the Pope has sent us his blessing!
(Conveyed by the Bishop of Nara)

‘Pray for the Pope’s intentions’
‘The Fires of Hell’, said Father Molloy,
While in the front row squinting at a boy,
Sat Kate who is a modest dove
Well-grounded in the perils that attend Free Love,
But not as nice as Peggy P.,
Who in one’s green days used to be
A good-time girl with risky males
And quite a dab at dubious tales:
In fact she held the bed quite dear,
But finished up with a skipping queer.
‘Three Hail Marys for the Conversion of Russia’.

3

There was thin blue light
Where some stars had upstaged
The clouding glass moon.
It annexed partially from the night
A fairly classic head, blonde hair,
A nape ending in shadows.

The rain had spiked us
Bone had gone to marrow-fat,
Eye to eye had grown unlike,
There were new hard pebbles in love's pockets.

The wind had towelled us,
Back to bone went attainable flesh
Limb grew to limb again familiar.
Lovers whisper their assuring axioms
Forget that the weather can catch them out,
Bodies come together as perfect strangers,
Terrified, mysterious, until the death in doubt.

4

Wake my love no more in nightmare,
Devil-goats should not be near,
When inside my arms I hold you,
Unless it is myself you fear.
Fear perhaps may be contagious,
Even when creatures are at peace:
Sometimes, child, I fear to lose you,
Since flesh, being weak, must beg release.

5

Flesh calls to flesh across the ramparts
Built by some spirit to protect its love,
But an aureate head may spin a halo
Persuading flesh that spirit has removed,
Tenanted another fleshy habitation
Where for a new death we're on probation.
Since each loss erases past possession,
We find that love has missed the bus,
And solitary, since we left the womb,
Romance up the night as personal doom.
There is some hope for little Peggy P.
But God of Love, is there any hope for me?

6

The Painted Men grow old,
Cold invades the veins
Where the blood of strangers pulses.
Clay triumphs over alchemy,
Brimstone guts the dressing-table.

But their plumes still wave
Above the screaming trees,
Wave their signal of unending love.
The glass moon, their complacent madame
Smiles, so tender, on their follies,
The stars shine for them
A macula especially.

But don't forget to pray for the Pope's Intentions,
Every single Sunday the P.P. mentions
Nuns, priests, abroad are very badly pressed
Bringing God to black babies and ensuring they're
dressed.
Yes, pray too for the destruction of the Reds,
For all poor occupants of unchaste beds,
For disgraceful dipsos, sods, and tarts
Joyces, Gides, and Jean-Paul Sartres.

And may Christ have mercy on us all.

[1948]

Wordsworth Was Right

'At eight-thirty a.m.
A Titian-headed girl
Said goodbye to her mother
Going down the steps
Through yellow light and the trees
Away to the beaches and May'.

'That's beautiful'. And the way she says it,
Her eyes all warmth, you'd think
She surely meant it.
What's the purpose of the lie?
What's the purpose of the great room,
Where the trailing cobweb glistens
And the ghosts tap their bones on the piano-lid,
Shuffle the sheets of Debussy, and the dust
Settling ...
Do you know what I mean?

What too' s the purpose of training American glory
Under subtle pretence of business and the like ...
Yet was that glory sweeter than the violets
Wet, wet violets sold in Stephen's Green,
Gentler, sharper, sharper than the candle-flame,
Candle guttering in Pembroke Road.

Listen people ...
Only he* could tell us the truth about it all:
The man who worried epic out of the sod
Stamped on the ashes till they glowed
The man who gleaned the lyric at the heart of the clod
The man who reaped what he sowed.

But how well we know, yes, what he would say,
Crashing through the cobwebs (lovely cobwebs!) to the
fine raw day.
Listen people …
'That's not poetry! Pure shite,
pure shite!'

'Yes, Patrick. That's very well put. But
Don' t you think …'
'The Muse is queer. She's like a goad.
Poetry's never written unless a man's
All on fire to do it, on fire with
Happi-
ness, on fire with
Sor-
row'.

O to get out of it
O to get out of it
O to get out of it
Or drink the Shannon dry!

Ah the eyes are warm again and the May days
Have come back to the room,
Crackling paper, spilling water,
Beautiful shades out of business.
Ah the eyes are warm again,
'Read us another one, John'.

'At four-thirty a.m.
A white-haired woman
Said goodbye to guests

Leading them down the steps
Through the night-stock fragrance
Out into the reaches of November'

[1948]

* Patrick Kavanagh

Ghosts in Marble

A worldly beauty by the world forgotten.
White gardens, golden domes and domes
scaled green and blue like a fish
And cypress and steps and cupids in gold and white plaster, and
garlands and groves of flowers,
Live doves and doves of clay that fly over the blue trains
And a marble head of Massenet and the sea laughing below:
Even the mountains think that you are dead.

I dreamed when I was a boy
That you were dead already, that the soul had died in you long ago;
And the girl at my side had the same dream.
You were a bauble, a griffin, a white armadillo
We said, and we looked at each other's eyes and laughed

That first night long ago
Long ago:
You were a plaything we said, a mad doll, a white wedding cake
Of honey and sugar and sugar plums and a heart
Of marble in your breast and a little tune
By Massenet you played
As you lay among roses in a gilded trellised box:
A casket of false gold alone in empty silken space
Painted to represent the sky. O well; it may be
We were right as we sat there—how young we were—
On azure straw chairs on a terrace
Under the dazzling umbrellas.

The world that lay at your feet
Was a world of flies:
Flies forever feasting off your sugar-marble flesh

So meticulously painted
And the sun and the moon shining down on you.

Maybe that first night we were right
And you were a gaudy fantasy of princes and of merchants.
But one day, suddenly, we fell in love with you
Desperately and bitterly as one can only fall in love
With negligence, with bright and wanton indifference.

And tonight I am looking at you out of the eyes of that old sterile love.
Tonight you are the loneliest thing in the world
And now you dream from dawn until night comes
And dream again and stir most pitifully
Under your sleep
And the flies no longer hover round you
To gnaw your heart away, and I think
That you are more bravely decked now than you ever were
In your bright past (beauty you never had)
More bravely decked, more elegant, more leonine,
Your flowers, your gloves, your jewels
Your painted eyes gold-lidded watching the sea forever.

The wheels still circle in your heart
Those polished glittering wheels that brought you fame and gold
But you no longer think of them, you are indifferent
To wheels and fame and gold alike
You have forgotten them as a man in his strength
Forgets his heart and all its traps and snares.
No, you dream of gold no more: your dream tonight
Is of small distant figures
That rise and fall, draw near and then recoil,
Your dream tonight is of dancers. You

Who have a myriad of tongues
Are dreaming tonight in the tongue
Of Russia, in the language
Of dancers.

Dance again, imperial dancers,
Although the stage is empty, the lights all dark
Dance. Here is level holy ground
Dance once again.
Your dreams are dense with ghosts:
Diaghilev walked on this ground long, long ago
The young Nijinsky by his side, docile, inexorable,
(Was it the Fool, grown divine, leading a King
Into the stormy dark?) And after
Nijinsky, Massine:
Meticulous, matriculative, limitless: then
Dolin came: the lonely slow-shot arrow of elegance
Passing leisurely out of the bow:
And Bakst, Picasso, Braque, Stravinsky,
Karsavina, Spessivtseva, Nikitina, Danilova—queens
Diamond-eyed, snow-sandalled, swift-flying
Among the shadows of other shadows
Of friends and lovers who are dead
And who walk here forever
Walk under starlight and the straight beams of the sun
Here in immaculate gardens on moon-blanched marble
And others still who whisper and laugh and talk
Of painting, of philosophy, of dancers
Forever young, because they are dead.

Oh you, my heart's love, you and I together
In loneliness of spirit in the loneliness of the gardens
We look at each other suddenly and laugh
And I remember that first night and that first laughter

Long ago
And the girl who is dead.
'A wedding-cake, no more ...'
O, forsaken beauty by the world forgotten,
O, elegant heart-breaking solitude,
Forgive the words: for how
Could we have understood you at the first swift breathless glance?
How could we have known?

It is quiet here: a white-footed silence
Steals past us like a sigh. I think that I could stay here forever
with you,
And all of us, we three, I and you and this white place,
Remembering that ancient laughter, that faintly mocking echo.
But suddenly you say, 'I cannot bear it
This dead and dreaming
Elegance, this ghost-filled moon-drenched
Worldliness: these are your ghosts, not mine,
Your ghosts, not mine ...'
And desire fills me
And fills these gardens
To share our ghosts with you as I would share
All things with you:
But my tongue lies like a stone,
I turn my eyes away and stare
Across the sea to where the moon
Cuts a bright road for her feet so light
Upon the water,
And I am glad that life is as it is
Although you think this place a tomb
As the mountains themselves have thought.

Only this place and I know this:
They are mistaken: the mountains are mistaken,

To dream of dancers underneath the moon
Is to eat of honey sweeter far
And more powerful far than death.

[Monte Carlo, 1948]

Second Letter: To Patrick Swift

Dear P.,
    This letter may explain better
    than words of the mouth,
    words, words, words,
    that soothed our drought
    through rain and stars,
    the mockery of dawn,
    we cold as the trees.

For you must keep in mind
that we are less than kin,
but more than kind, for

    While you were ranting your lyceum lines
    careering the vaults of your glittering dooms,
    bleeding at the heart from paper knives—
    I have my nuances and Chekovian glooms—
    But we were both mummers, and so we got on.

    Mine was a mime of lime-scent and heart-break
    quiet, frail, imbecile, thirsty for applause—
    and O you knew that and nurtured me, because—
    Thespis's children stick together
    in sunlight and shower and weather
    when the proud rose must surely fall,
    thrown on a dump with all the rest of the trappings,

        the split gold tights
        the ragged brocade gown
        the mothy ermine choker
        the sweet tinsel crown
    and our cascades of pasten jewels,
    bright as tears,

worthless as tears,
your tears,
my tears.

Yes, mine was a mime of lime-scent and quiet heart
yours one of cypresses, and blood on the snow
but we both were mummers and didn't care to know,

to realize,
to dig,
to pick away the paint,
to clutch the hand lovingly
around the white skull.
Skull last seen in the dead of night
or glimpsed at waking in the submarine light,
skull precious ivory,
to be kissed and touched tenderly ...

As you may have noticed
the games are done
and I for one, my friend, am very tired.
I must confess, too, I find it hard
not to have regrets,
for years spent in plays
so unworthy of our talents.

It will be difficult to adapt ourselves to ordinary life. And of course we' ll always be peculiar, rearing the head, pouting the lips, stancing the body, when a stranger comes into the room. You know that as well as I do.

Yours,
John Jordan.

[Dublin, 1948]

A Seduction of the '40s

She was a fine girl, amber, supple,
He was a real fine boy, long-lashed.
She said to him one night
        (When they were ending a chat
        About Pico—him with the Golden Hair)
She said to him one night:
'Come up, come see me one night'
The trouble was they both had brains.
So he went up to see her one night.
She had a very nice flat
With lamp-shades designed special
And a photo signed *le gach deá-ghuí*
By an Irish actor and rows and rows of books.

There was a balcony too and they looked down into the
        garden
And he said, 'You know, darling,
Your breasts, I mean bosom, is like apples.'
She said, 'Don't give me that crap.'
They'd both seen Bogey in *Casablanca.*

She was a great girl and they had six gins with orange.
She said, 'I do think you've got a tiny waist for a man.'
So it went on until 2 a.m.
He stood up, took off his jacket,
Went to the window and said,
        'Let us walk out where people look out
        On trees and flowers and wonderful affairs,
        And never look in on death and sin,
        Excrement of the unspeakable mind,
        Insolent bully',
Or words to that effect.

And she said, 'Gee'.
He sat down beside her, put his hand on her bosom.
It opened out to him
Not at all like pippins.
She said, 'You'll have to leave.'
So it went on to 3 a.m.
He stood up, took off his shirt.
Dixit: Now that the sleeping time is come
And love's musk scents the air
Let us lie down and cease to wear
Our bottoms out in foolish talk,
Masochistic jabbing.
Dixit: I don't like the use of that word 'bottom'.
Dixit: It's about time we
Learnt that the heart's no pincushion.

And then, you know, he put out the light,
And they went to bed and were unhappy ever after.

[Dublin, 1948-49]

Eclectic

Sweet Sacrament
Divine transmutation
Flesh into spirit.

Rubble of garments
Unwashed teacups
Gibbering danger
à la Graham Greene

(Thomas McGreevy
Thirty years ago
Gnashed his Catholic teeth
At our bitch of a world)

(Thomas McGreevy
O'er the Bank of Ireland
Heard unearthly music
Passing westwards)

'What are those yellow …'
'O they're chrysanthemums',
The music began
In a phalanx of flowers.

We went west
At two in the morning.
We came back at five
And the music died.

Sweet Sacrament
Divine transmutation
Spirit into flesh.

[1948-49]

Trahison Des Clercs

for Pearse Hutchinson

Some people that you know,
An old woman peeved by defeat,
A sex-meshed codger
Whose heart does not go,
A subtle sunshine boy, one sleepy eye on
'every main chance',
Have abused you, all three in a row.
And I, because of a secret low allegiance
To a six-hour day, a cushioned chair,
Enough cash to be able to save,
Have been silent.

[Dublin, 1949]

An Imaginary Biography

1

He loved much in his youth,
Drank deeply from the wine
Vendible tepid summer evenings,
Those Georgian days in Kildare Street.

But at fifty,
His sisters nibbled their veils,
Splashed in their sherry,
Let crumbs of *Marie* biscuits
Drop, cling, in the red flannel
They wore for their chests.
Frail, merry, unaware of hell,
They were full of requests
That he'd take a wife, so
Keep the stock alive, for
They had married one and all,
Grown grey mice, and small,
Known only the rind of motherhood:
Julia, Sally and Rose
Bought cousins' babies clothes,
And dandled changelings
At their player breasts.
On the whole they were distraite
And after thirty years
Had grown somewhat tired
Of waiting their helpmates
Eat, sleep, shave,
Hearing them guffaw,
Drunkenly weep, of

Lying by blocks of lard,
Cold, dry, hard,
Cold as their seed.

2

Year by year they went,
Julia, Sally and Rose,
With crocuses and happy rain,
A minimum of mourning,
An excess of whiskey, and
Their husbands said they'd loved them.
But still he was single:
Happy but for a thin pain
That caught him in the small
Of his back—that was all.

He took to gin and frolics,
He read enormous tomes,

For he was a scholarly man,
Knew Greek, dreamed of Japan.
They all said: 'He is failing'.
How could he have health
Scooping tinned salmon in a stuffy room?
He would wear his heart out on drink,
Die on the road without a priest
To speed him to the brink
Of plum-blossom land where *Iosagán* is so pretty.

They were wrong.
Dying he heard the hot song
Of thrushes from the Sisters' garden.

In a warm lavender room
With window blinds called fawn,
A flowery chamber-pot and every dawn,
The loony chime of a landing-clock,
He dreamed the journey of his days
Glancing out at all the ways
He'd met with beauty:
Shriven, he saw beneath the skin
Of those he'd loved and lusted,
Could not quite consider sin
Moments when he'd trusted,
Staked his immortal soul
On an eyelash flicker,
Rose to glory on the pediment of despair.

One dawn that Spring, plum-blossom invaded his room,
The crazy clock shrilled through the percolated gloom,
And then onwards his peace was quite extraordinary.

[Dublin, 1950]

Homage to the Pseudo-Jansenius

The faithful, quite rightly, will not listen to reason.
From the hubris of innocence they know
The path to be as narrow as the gate.
They forsake all forms of richness
Since wavering for creatures
Most certainly entails being late,
Breaking and entering the preserves of the elect,
The pinched, fearful of fantasy,
Disdainful of cakes and ale,
The true passengers.

All the rest of it is maculate:
Clerical quip and liberal mind,
Perspectives of eternity which we're told
Art can find—
Christian Plato, the stretching by fly boys of Thomas the Ox.

The rub lies with the distant honeys,
Sienese cheek-bones, Buonarotti hips,
Challenge the Rock of Ages,
Damned by tenderness, we turn asterisked pages,
Will never, though, live, adore, be luminous
Out of this world and time.

[Dublin, 1950]

Non Dicam

The decision has been made: I shall not tell you.
Fear, toilet-trained now, has spliced my tongue.
Fear of same débâcle as other loves' recitals,
Nasty and brutish the Leviathan of disdain.

As things are at least the knowledge,
The presence of a friable decision,
Feathery images of sesamatic words
Make tolerable a yen for sweet permission.

But, dear thing, must I attend
A quarantine of a lustrum
Because the hound pounces on to its desire?
Can nothing in my bearing
Key you to the cypher,
Pull out the bloody plug before there's fire?

But the decision has been taken
Resolve must not be shaken
By casual affection in your tones.
I must feed in isolation
Prune ramblers of elation
Snip all Aves and Vales
And breast-buds when I see you all alone.

Vingt ans après
In clockish time some sixty hours,
Tongue has jerked the splice,
Has opened pain.
The decision has been broken
Though to you I have not spoken.

The mines are flooded, Christ,
It's dark again.
I must build a raft from flotsam,
The vomit in the belly
Time may clear away,
Mens insana, too, will perhaps be sane.
I sight already wrack, suitably inadequate,
I'll work it out in shanties,
And brave again skin-diving in the main.
Vingt ans après
In clockish time some sixty hours,
I have found coral, amber, excrement,
Armour for another soft or squally day.
For which I am truly thankful,
And can hail you, O my dear,
Salve.

[Dublin, 1950]

Gerard Dead 1

They told him at school about Voltaire,
How the Jesuits made much of him,
And the bright boy
Died a most horrible death.

Missioners from the pulpit warned him of pride,
Which might imperil his deathless soul,
Worse, worse than Tophet, the joy
Of choiring God be withheld.

Brothers, missionaries, a Russian salad of clerics,
Drove home His bones and His Bloody Side,
His child-days were enlightened by baroque images
Of how gruesomely his Saviour Christ had died.

The horrible and disgusting details of His death
Did not mark him, nor the pathos of His Birth.
The game was worth no candles,
Candles to his gentle mother,
Heaven, if anywhere, lay in bread and wine of earth.
But some candle near the heart was real,
Lit Gethsemene, lit Calvary,
Lead him to kneel.

[Dublin, 1950]

Love Poem

'…ma douce Permission'
— Apollinaire

The sky stilettoed by the hooked branch I've seen
For the first time and silver sea-shell patterns on the roof,
The chubby crocus in the cocoa clay:
O love, one further proof.

The real arrived, grief's bunting trails along the wind,
The ruffian birds that wake me no more pain:
Love's yahoo, I will paint with them the whole world rose,
O love, my gentle proof, if it remain?

Then soon with my new sight we'll walk along the powdered ways
To the inn where the peacocks pierce the summer days,
Where the air all weightless gold will beat upon our cheeks,
And time will seem the substance that the dreamer seeks.

[Dublin, Spring/Summer 1951]

An Old Letter

To begin with and in a manner of speaking
We live in the trenches.
You are on leave in the sunlight.
Your wine glitters because it seems unending
And is unending, the heart at peace being cretinous,
Careless as child in cinema darkness.
                                        I say 'Careless'
But knowing you, knowing
The craters that lie before you even beneath
Crisp waters when you drift amber,
Darkness that snuffs scarlet green and golden rockets
I should say 'Careful'.
And I see you with care, with tenderness,
Swallowing the ruby on diapered terraces
Slowly and grave entering the sheets,
Your careful rapture as you explore again love's valleys,
The mysterious woods where peace should be.

But yet you are on leave in the temporary sunlight,
I cannot expect you, but do with all my heart,
To figure the oil and the dirt, the pus-smells,
Our bloody dreams, not of the temporary sunlight
Nor the deathless ruby, nor love's valleys
Nor mysterious woods where peace should be,
But wood-glow and tea-cups, door against the rain,
The wind noises, the dependable window-panes.
I want you to know how we wake
To the stench of tears, bloody sweat,
Eyes, heels, sore from the narrow patrols,
Lips smarted from incautionary kisses.

Perhaps that's taking it to the fair,
For we are not really in the trenches.
How you'll smile when I tell you:
No oil, no blood, no uncommon dirt here
But gradated greenery
And tranquil at the top of the garden
A green cushion, an orange chair,
A woman, a man, a boy, like you in the sunlight
But screened by pied lilac.
To end with and in a manner of speaking
I love you and we live in the trenches.

[London, 1951]

The Chime

for B.G. Achong

Talking is as bad as not talking.
Silence is as perilous as speech.
Between the chinks of speech
Falls the hail of silence.

Telling is as bad as not telling.
Confession posits standards,
Fouls up the wells of grief,
Each glance turns hazardous.

Vision is as bad as fancy.
Certain waiting as hard on the heart
As a squinting vigil with a clock.

Say then there's no difference
Between good-will and good-bye.
Quote deep sea and devil.
Say then there's no difference:
But the difference is music,
A class of chime,
Heard at all times, at all places.

[Dublin, 1951]

Gerard Dead 2

i.

Words, lint on wound, unwritten dedications,
Surrogate feeling, cramp in the night.
Still the true misery exists, burgeons,
The glittering ache of more fortunate
Lovers, mothers, authentic brothers:
Words dislocate local necessary pain.

ii.

Take those tulips festering in the death-room,
Crucial blossoms, they celebrate the episode well-played,
This wood where we mourn the face we have made:
This is no dead boy but a Trojan shade,
At very least an infant from castellated Spain.

iii.

Words will not redeem our poor marionette,
The toy horse, wicker shoes, mauve light
Where Dietrich inspects, all plumes and ermine,
The mended linen where they have you lain.

vi.

The facts could not be a plain dead boy,
Who crooned in gutters with marbles in his fist,
Who perchance with innocence worked out a tryst,
Kept it through dog-days of beckoning hell,
Hurled Satchmo back at the passing bell.

v.

But O brother mine your false
Brother begs that you
Intercede, plead, give the info'
On what happened.
Beg salt for my eyes,
Gripe for my bowels.

[London-Oxford, 1951-53]

Song

Gone are my goblin and his fairy queen
To the shimmering city where I should have been
Had a hobgoblin not fed upon my heart
Gobbled all up a very big part,
Left me to cry on an English Green,
In the shimmering city where I should have been

[London, 1951]

Your Mouth

I was thirsty
and I found the wine cup
and I drank from it
and now I am lonely for
that old craving.

I was hungry
and I found the bread of life
and I ate of it
and now I am lonely for
that old emptiness.

I was lonely
and I found your mouth
and I kissed it
and I am lonely now only for
death.

[Dublin, 1953]

Fourth Letter: To David Posner

Dear D.,

Because with you
Big Daddy, Justice, booms again,
Because with you the harvest of flails
Seeded by we little ones that confuse Cross and Tree,
Is again believable: I write to you.

You have known, I believe, the queasiness of Mass-time,
The temptation of solitude in the afternoon,
Nostalgia for unexplored elm-dark gardens,
That comes in with the First of Sacred June,
'The starveling is fed on Sunday mornings,
The sacred mops up the leaky profane',
Yet *grand siècle* maxims, airs from Poulenc,
Shoot across the fresh interior rain.
You who would 'like to be forsaken
By tears that do not count'
Are right to have none of me
For whom the heart-strings are apron-strings,
Each romantic picnic a return
To summer-days, white lilac,
Sand-castles that, lackaday, seemed durable.

But don't bother your noddle,
I've long since mastered the role of *Désolé,*
(I've been quite a flop as D*é*sir*é*),
I've learned from repertory the way to handle
Needless prompts from Will Hay.
Still, because with you, that old bags Mercy
Sets up her stall in the High,

Cherubim and Seraphim
Are again believable: I write to you.
Believe me, that alone is why.

[Oxford, 1953]

In the Nine Winters

In the nine winters of our discontent
We unflesh pity for a thorned motive
In new departures from required perfection,
Groping for succour of unsteady images
From childhood, death-bed, private blackness.
With these we sow the creepers of our giving,
Master our crabbish scuttle from taking.
'So long, God, and my Galatea
I've just noticed my heart is breaking'.

So, on we travel to the next shipwreck
Followed by the Fisherman's inland bird.
The creature's voluntary skewers the elegy
Sung in a fathom's knowledge of sinking,
Drowned for a hand of yellow coarse hair,
Marinated for a daub of love.
Dead lovers rise from new shipwrecks
Often and most amiably are drowned:
For their nine winters they dream the knowledge
That cock and gull make the same sound.
But Galatea and my God,
I'm presently waking.
Have you lost your senses?
My heart is breaking.

[Oxford, 1954]

'Entre Chat Et Loup'

for Quentin Stevenson

Cry no more with cat and wolf
Roam no more about the gulf
Where the gallant go to dive
And being dead come back alive.

Send away the hearthside cat
Starve the wolf that did not bite.
Dive deep down for what you lack
Being alone you may come back.

Leave the twilight while you may
Find the day beyond the day
All that light that sharpens form,
Beats the wild thing back to norm.

Death is where they cannot give:
You must ask for grace to love
Far away from cat or wolf,
Dive quite alone into the gulf.

[Oxford, 1954]

Self-Portrait: Oxford

At peace in sunlight
Pinchbeck Greco come to rest,
He is disfettered from his native world,
Peaceable in gold.

Never, he dreams, again
The cool guests, the invited quarrels,
The moons that look on no harvest.

[August 1958]

One Who Was Not Invited to the Opening of the Joyce Tower Complains Bitterly

They came:
Jesuits, judges, Telefís jokers,
Visiting firemen, Cork pipe-smokers,
Monumental patrons, U.C.D. wives:
Time, O you beast you, despite your worst forgives.

They goggled:
Columnists, socialites, jolly old pals,
Round-the-clock drinkers, Trinity gals,
Play okay-ers, the Minister, *haute couturieres*:
Time, O you *pup* you, has made you one of theirs.

They guzzled:
Doctors, lawyers, departmental bosses,
BBC balladmen, drawn by lucky horses,
Socialists, capitalists, Fianna and Fine:
Time, O you *fiend* you, has put you back in line.

They went:
Piling into taxis, limousines and growlers,
Titivating tipsily the afternoon's howlers:

'God, it must have cost
Scott a lot of lolly.
Tell me now boys,
Does he leave the key with Dolly?'

But, O you man you,
It was different in ’twenty-two
When few but Cons were pro
And most of the rest were anti.

[Blanchardstown, 1962]

Tidings from Breda

i.

Sweating in my underclothes in Breda,
False Greco face mosquito-swollen,
A couple of thoughts laid a
Hand on me: indecent assault
On soul.

ii.

One man said, kindly Machiavel:
'Others have done what you have done,
Squandered talents, gone in for fun,
Outgrown wild oats, made a success'.
In so many words, 'Get out of the mess'.
Spoken very wisely, not very well.

iii.

Wisdom smokes from the unstaked.
Good direction is morsed from the blinkered.
But, mind you, I'm inclined
To think that an earlier season
Might have found me more receptive
When *couilles* and caul were of sturdier kind.

iv.

Everyman has a singular future.
Mine is failure. I'd better admit it.
It may suit you, wise men and bright girls
To wish on me flecks of glory.
But I am I. Alone I know
The facts. Jordan's Book of Records
Would shake you. My locks are gory.

v.

Barren, barren, barren:
The cicadas sing.
I've done my best these days to forget:
Lent my razor to Joaquín
(O, the fruiting fig trees outside my window)
Discussed aesthetics with Maria Antonia,
High above the City of the Virgin:
I brought lost loved ones gossip and whiskey,
She crescented with child,
He waxed proud, bronzed, mythical,
Drunk Free Cubas with *La Barba*,
Heard, told, tales of Señora Nati,
Was dropped at Prici's by Toni and Mati,
('You are too tall?,' said Mati,
'You must rest more', said Nati)
At four o'clock the roosters wake me.

vi.

Some good may come of this:
High above the City of the Virgin
La Barba Catalanized
The least favoured cygnet of
The Swan of Coolgreany.
An omen: light flickers,
Failure of power. Unlike that Swan
I'm slow at the go. Yet
Though he cackle at my mewling
I will not shy from his crackling.
Swans, one's told, have songs.
Pavlova bit the dust.

vii.

I have been cruel for twenty years
(Or nearly), douched desires
Of undesired, homely, mad, thick,
Pot rejecting kettle:
That club-footed Yank I unhearted
That breastless girl who
On a go-cart
Pushed her brats across Europe
Plucked lemons for snotty faces
Plunged the stallions of madness
Through immemorial groves,
Who, locked up, did not die,
Came back along the lemon track.
I would straighten, Club Foot,
I would breast you, little Carter.

viii.

I descend to vermouth and dominos.
Tonight the rain thrashes indoors
Chronic viewers who forget to drink
The fig trees are desolate.
Supper is late.
Catalan, ten years in Brazil
(Where the nuts come from)
Tells of Irish friend Wilson,
Higgins, Campbell, who hated the English.
Do I?
'The past is the past'.
Deny self. Liberal lies are bonny.
Heart whispers,
'What a whopper, honey'.
Past is not past.
More than the blessed air
It pumps into us wakefulness
Sustains ache for lilac
Long since swept down the drains.

ix.

Mother Church carries her burnt babies
Reclaimed drunk suckles delerium
Happy daddy pats his joyful solitaires
Nobel prizeman serves in trance *disjecta membra*
The fruiting fig trees croon their Master's Curse.
How could it be otherwise?

x.

Sprung from credulous loins
I'm partial to miracles.
It is not beyond the cards
(The smell of dung invades)
Fifty may find me cock
Stock and barrel successful,
Wife, kiddies, house, coins,
Many visible garlands about me.
But I say my future is failure.
Late in the night of
April Eighth
Nineteen Hundred
Sixty Three
I saw it.
(Master of the Short Line, forgive me.)

xi.

Harden, Leland, John and Con,
Dickie, Paddy dear, Dara and the Swan,
Were among those who assisted at the Wake.
Take it, pet, from me, that was it
No resurrection or *natividad.*
O love it was truly all very sad.
(O Nati you should have been there!)
No rebudding of spent branches
No messages of hope for the peoples
Only jaded *collage* of my pat tricks
(Pardon treey bridge, swallowy garage)
And perhaps for Carroll's Special some stories:
Death at the Bridge of the Ball
By Juan Christi.

xii.

Lights out. 'Franco, Franco!'
On Mont-Seny thunder fee-fa-fums,
Mongrels, pied, black, do their David.
Rain fifes, thrums and drums:
Good Lord, the peace of failure.
Calm brow, cool throat, bathed limbs,
Season for the lamb, a complex beast
When you've known paper lions:
My bestiary is for sale, my love,
There are for you slashing reductions.
But may I suggest that crook-necked nag:
Give him a carrot, some hay,
Sugar at Christmas and major feasts.
If you have to bury him
Let it be far from the furious Swan.
If you have to skin him,
You may find a boy of ten
A-jingle with medals step-dancing
Tears to his mother's eyes
(She was a school-teacher before her marriage—
This was her youngest). But
Perhaps an old nag's heart
Can take no engraving.

xiii.

Toni has come with a stranger.
Cointreau has the texture of dew.
Toni's eyes are smudged purple.
I pay the bill and through the moted air
We descend to the City of the Virgin.

[Breda, Cataluña, 1963—Dublin, 1970]

Excoriations on Mont-Seny …

Cocks crow all day on Mont-Seny :
What fowlish pleasure, what inexpressive pain?

White, blue, butterflies,
Pastel leaves,
Light on low water
Lassoing rock.

Broken cartwheels I have seen in Ireland.
But blackberries here are small and bitter.

Guardia Civil rinses mouth with soda water.
Unlike mate leaves rifle at the wall.

Rusted white church
Looks over cock
Butterfly blackberry
Water cartwheel
Guardia Civil rock
Me
O why the rifle?

[Breda, 1963]

Athens

Girls and boys from Antipodes
And west of the Appalachians
I desiderate your vigour, your all-seeing eye,
No more, no less, than your chimera.
Daunted by Acropolis
Promethean by daylight
Faraday'd in nightlight
I sit in the Square, redundant,
And read *Felix Holt.*

[August 1965]

A Minor Complication

High above the city of the Three Cities
The memories coalesce. Mustapha
Fiddler with electricity, stealer of bottles,
Donor of cabbages. Post-midnight knocks.
Rocks hurled by children the Prophet
Suffered to come onto him. Hassan,
Camel meat, but was he truly *marocain*?
Suliman, bearer of wine and olives,
Incarnation of Islamic mischance,
His friend Bakush whose memories
Regrettably embrace the *palais de danse*,
Not least the Neighbour with his methedrine,
That other ruffian and his Jacqueline.

Never again the trek to Armando's
Never again at six in the morning
The call to prayer for arid Christian buffs
Never again this afternoon of tolerable peace
When the world is governed by doves.
No vulture can take this from me.

Detail the objects on the desk.
Twenty years ago I saw that Venus,
('There she is', said Liam Ó Briain)
Seventeen years ago that Copenhagen nude,
('Get her, dear', said someone rude)
Ash-trays, the clutter of work,
An orange, Desmond's 'Artemis', lean
Script that may survive the Vandals.
A match box from Malta, *A Lonely Voice*,
All the mystery of Islam. I am too old to alter.

We do not eat *Chateaubriand*
We discuss the man.
Pushing forty in North Africa
One drops names like Goethe,
Goes on to discuss the gloomy Dane
How Rousseau might have poured into him
The desire to confess:
'Those who mess with God are not officers nor gentlemen'.
Which brings me to a pose.
Being a minor complication a friend's life is trying,
God's minor complications happen when we are dying.

But screw the doggerel.
In the middle of the journey
I see no dark wood

Only unchanging laurels
Torrents of doves
Hurtling against the wind.

Philoctetes will be my guide
I will wear my pus like alabaster.

[Tripoli, Libya, 1969]

Forewarned

i.

Do you think we should measure
Quality of life by prestige of stimuli?
"The power of cheap music,
'Noël, Noël'?"
Ought we to anatomise if salt
Is spilt over Parma violet memories,
The seed tremor with bifurcated yen?

"Better give thanks for all feeling,
Tear in the eye for Mother Machree
Loin shudder for lost napes
Surrogate plastic when there's no filigree."

ii.

Sex they tell us is not lust
Angelic matrons tell the lost
One-night passion turns to dust:
Sex is not a handled thigh,
Holy fathers fence the gash.
I look you in the candid eye:
Sweet Jesus, if the love-lech takes me.

iii.

And it did: and heart now croaks
And ravens, and round my thigh
There's a scelus of ragwort.
My pillow is often wet
My tongue licks the pustules
Of squandered kisses: stains of passion
Unseen to strangers blur my pupils.
All we can hope for now is
The Removal of the Remains.

[Dublin, 1969]

A Guest of the Dean's

for Austin Clarke

i.

Great Dean, invigilator of our loves and liberties,
Here is United Ireland. The burrs of thirty-two counties
Stick in my heart. That cool twelve thou' has
Bought me fraternity. We are all experts here.
Schizophrenics, depressives, alcoholics, pathics,
Some elated like the Blessed Saints, others
Withdrawn to who knows what red hell or
Candid heaven, all are duly elected members,
Academicians who may never resign, signatories
Of the treatment.
    Woe to the formulators of empty oaths.
They may know again the quality of shipwreck,
Watch with eyes like piss-holes in the snow
Manannán betray his tasty kinship with Moloch,
Be trapped at Calais by the mad Irishwoman
Who thinks she lives among niggers: sniggers
Should be the rhyme. Madness is no laughing
Matter. Though some here laugh like madmen.
    In remote farms tongue-less bachelors
Stash barley and juniper against demonic thirst.
Forget their caches and drive mad through
St. Patrick's snake-less night. The sheebeen is
Mother's arms. The paps are horny
With plenty. The cocks crow. Swollen
Teats are dumb. Last night their
Master was 'fierce lonely'.
    'Have you a drinking problem ?'

'Well, I suppose, like the other lads.' Your
Toms, Dicks and Harrys are here, great Dean.
You gave your lolly to found our first democratic
Institution. Paudeen and Algernon rub minds.

ii.

Some who have gone from soft to hard
Have been warned by Nurse against lonely pathic.
The Eye of Heaven blazes on the strollers
In the Gardens of *Welldorm*: did the bats
Come in middle of night? The cats tie themselves
To your body? The scimitars castrate you?
The *Artane* Band parades among the roses.
The Legion *of Gardenal* inspects the dahlias.
(Great Dean, your people, yours and mine, call them day-lias)
Surmontilised, the clock-golfers beat the rap.
Cuchullains, tight-pantsed, hand the ball,
Mini-skirted Deirdres ply the racquet.
They do not pray for you at Mass, great 'Dane',
As your people called you.

When the Host is raised
They think not of your Liberties or Loves,
Each soul dead-set for personal salvation
Accepts as natural bounty your crazed wish,
Forgets the torment in the ears and heart,
Would surely damn a man with two women.
Our democracy has its fascists.
The love of man and man is 'dirt'. Among the
Roses and the dahlias as the all-seeing Eye
Blinks alight I'm told it's 'worse than besti-itis'
(A notable coinage from the County of Laois).
At Courtown on holiday
Ex-inmates meet. Do they discuss
Heights of *Valium*, Scrolls of *Librium* or
Those strolls in the Gardens of *Welldorm*?

iii.

United Ireland has its constipation problems.
Immemorial castor oil still has its uses.
Some of our citizens like Martin, François, yourself great 'Dane',
Make us privy to their cloacal mysteries.
Bowels without compassion confuse thought,
Spanner the works: pique, bad temper!
    All the rage is regularity.
The men on the moon must be punctual.
Many will bay if poet's image is violated
While *Welldorm* or *Doriden* is in the saddle.
Insomniacs, inviolate to patent sleep, will
Bless their sickness if they catch the telly
While others dream of Bacchus' sloppy lips,
Ganymede's slim-fit hips, Venus' abounding bosom.
    Tomorrow our democracy
Will drop marmalade, slobber porridge,
Let fry cool, tea tar, valued butt incinerate.
We are all experts here. Elated and withdrawn
Will find the Moon their common ground.
Boozers will start out of pre-planned temptation,

The sick of Eros will goggle at heart's craters revealed.
You, great 'Dane', chained on your parthogenetic rock,
May remember when the Moon had its liberties,
When the Liberties had a Moon and a Man in it.
Pray for us, reluctant Prometheus. Remember
The House of which you are Father.

[Dublin, 1969]

The Feast of St. Justin

i.

Removed to another part of the forest of symbols
(Latin me that, me Trinity scholard)
Iveagh's cornucopia no longer rich to hand,
In fine chilled air I see Wellington gone amber
And mind skirls with aislings of Pakenhams base and blessed
And primary that Passionist Thomas one.
My thoughts are pious. In stricter air,
In perfectly inviolate insomnia,
Ego ceases to self-canonize, play Everyman,
Florentine, those creatures that gibe or whatever
In William Blake. Wellington's egg-shell now.
Match-box at stake.

ii.

There's a fine fling to the term magnanimity,
The open-palmed gest, the butter of gold,
Old wine, sapient chunter over Montaigne,
I yet in this chillier air see more virtue in forgiveness,
Wonder at its almighty gradations.
Christ asking Dad to forgive Gentile and Jew;
This is immediately graspable, fist in the pale
Of ponderables, despotic and heraldic fact.
But Mary forgiving Jesus for his brusquerie,
This, my children, is of the minutiae of daily experience.
I will not understand that eighth dolour of hers
Unless there be primal mystery in forgiveness.

iii.

Once
From a grianán of Noel Browne's
I saw an orange bird
And blessed the gaudy paraclete
That chose to pass my window.
Apollonian rapers have no power
Over minds saddened by maddered flesh,
Dethroned eyeballs, skewered genitals,
The minutiae, my children, of daily experience.
Will these have their part in the inordinate forgiveness?
Will Picasso be forgiven for his pretty white dove?
Will no account be taken of Iscariot's love?

iv.

Peace of mind is greatest treasure.
That Passionist Thomas one, hollowed and hallowed,
    was allowed
The gluttony of blessings. Spirit can be rapacious.
But to have one's unpaid clothes secreted,
Not to be permitted that spiky air, that chill at the feathers,
Is indignity, gross though mandatory, loonish if regular.
Religio Medici is a queer text. *Religio medicorum*
Sancti Patricii best known to themselves.
Will they be forgiven for refusing the Host?
Will they get a glim of the Seraphim,
A look-in when the Hosannas are vaunted?
Facit indignatio versum: but I have no spleen against them.

v.

I suppose like the rest they'll be forgiven:
Hitler and Picasso, Dali and Franco,
Frank Ryan and Stephen Hayes: the lot.
Including the Butcher whose fleerings
Will be part of my punishment. Leering
Torturers are part of my daymares.
He'll stump around the American circuits,
Not know he's a non-figure, a cypher,
And darkling in my bosom loom to gay madness.
I will not be part of the inordinate forgiveness
Since I cannot forgive the pride of thickness
Nor Newman's gentleman adjusting the batteries.

vi.

Forgive us this day
Our daily bread
Our ration of rice
Our peck of spice
Wrapped up in *The News of the World.*
All humanity's there, including the beast.
God will be good to the pure and the troglodyte,
God will be guardian to the plain and erudite.

God will be grand to us all if we accept
The vast unreason of forgiveness.
And let's face it, dears, that means we must all
Sit down to barbecue with the Johnsons and yacht-
Yickety-yacht with Onassis: there's a limit to exclusiveness.
O, I pray though, that some primal mystery in forgiveness
May redeem it: Have mercy, O Lord, on forgiveness.

Letter to Paul

i.

Baptised by St. John of God,
Faith severely tested at Belmont
Tutored at Westminster on London's old sod,
Delivered, pre-packaged, to the Moated Grange,
None of this can have been pleasant.
Did you maybe turn a page here
Where Iveagh's vats dottle the thick of Summer
And their black nectar (also their harpy cousins)
Are seen only in electric box or silly-billy mirage?
        Or were you here in Winter
When the vivid casques were silvered
The pear-tree nude and unashamed
When gravel squelched and P.T. was
Always indoors, graceless concertina ballet?
No, none of this can have been pleasant.

ii.

But in nineteen hundred and sixty seven
Barely zoned, you took to an untormented sea,
No longer alone, made over by Eros' liturgy,
Coarse salt for your tongue, for your loins opal foam.
Others, purblind lepidopterists, holes in their nets,
Pursued phantom moths over almond sands,
Trekked icing-sugar wastes, were tardily sprung
By the Great Hunter (one gets tired of that Hound).
He whom they call the noon-day devil
Others Asmodeus, caught us over the barrel,
Our current accounts dry, tax-gatherers converging,
Our credit dinged, our public images, dear me,
quite blotched.

iii.

I should speak only for my thousand and one selves,
For a self scissored from its native motley,
Life-caul sold for coils of old rope,
Imprints, signatures, conjectured dates, intaglios
On lacquer, sub-structure weeviled,
Castors squeaky: scholarship old Pollux.
For a self stripped of its supernatural drag,
Taste of wafer seasonal like rheum,
Whiff of incense in my city's streets, unscheduled prayer,
'God keep me safe, Mother Mary this night
Don't let it happen, let there be light.'
For self, ah no, 'selves' period: fast glaziered
When diamonds had broken and entered,
Nineteen or nine lives I.O.U.'d *in saecula,*
Splintered trusts, squatters' wrongs,
Wings of a buff flapping a dowdy empyrean.

iv.

Hateful ego: this is for you
And the fairy woman and the child
Called for the bride of Axel.
Man, woman, child, are Trinity,
Semen, blood, milk, a binding mixture.
I'd like to think your perhaps unattractive scrap
(A week before death Borstal Boy described
His new-born as a sausage: he was brandied)
At the right time herself a Conceiver
Of Trinities, in her own right a Blessed Person.
To that end, but not necessarily so:
May she have teeth that are neat but discreet,
May she have limbs engaging but fleet,
May she have eyes fathomless but kind,
May she have flesh that will stay unlined,
May her heart never over-step the mark,
—Do I mean that? no, let her know the lark
In the clear air of her first mornings,
Even nightingales heard in Berkeley Square
Are not to be sniffed at, if she's a woman
At all: she will be the better for human love,
But, like drink, not too much of it.

v.

May she not know an adder in her breast,
May she not host a demon as her guest,

May she not find an onion in her glass,
May she not marry a good-natured ass,
—Do I mean that? no, let her learn that 'mine'
In the language of mortals is
Dubious currency, a tricky decibel,
Still, not to be sniffed at if she's a woman
At all: she may not be the worse for human love.
I find this letter, Paul, hard to end:
The skein of madness tends to unravel
Into boleros Ravel never dreamed of:
But from my chambers in James's Street
I am yours, Man, Woman, Child, Trinity.

Heimweh

To have *Heimweh* for a madhouse
To half-hear Jaime when he discusses Sender
(Chiefly *cosas amorosas y sexuales*)
To, in short, be a member of an institution
For medicated vegetables, is not a solid preparation
For the infrequent 16A and the price of vegetables,
I mean vegetables for real, the moulting cauliflower,
The lecherous carrot, the hearted cabbage,
The mosquish onion, the shrewish radish,
All the bounty men dig in plots,
Not excluding the unchaste celery,
And the parsnip made famous by Yeats,
Whose *Heimweh* for Innisfree is pretty suspect.
But then one suspects them all,
Du Bellay, Donncha Rua, whoever
Was responsible for 'Galway Bay' frightening
Manannán on the way to Liverpool,
Dread accompaniment to puke and puddle,
The heart of exile stinking of stale stout:
Porter had a Synge to it, but not bottled,
Inclement stout that loosens liver and lights.
Ah, the relief of Liverpool and the great clock tower.
There are thousands and thousands who've had *Heimweh* for Liverpool
But to have it for a madhouse is at least invidious,
To love fiercely the faces of the violently unhappy,
Rhoda the hippopotamus whose daughter's a bitch,
Young snapper who's handy at his wrists,
Minds with just that one mote in them,
The thread that coarsens the turnip:
Such love is certifiable, the lover a fink,
A mind pickled with Gaelic salads,

Unchristian sauces, unfree libations
Fit for Romany, Lascar, Pink,
But surely not for one whose hand
Has cracked the ice in the Holy Water stoup,
Who has stooped and crackled muscles
Before the Ark of the Most High;
But, saving thought: whatever of Him was man
Decidedly was finkish; our iconologists
Depict him long-haired, he lay about
Not only in the Garden, went in for love-feasts,
Suffered the ministrations of tarts. His Father
Put him through most drastic therapy:
At a time like that, resurrectionary thoughts were not, I'd say, a balsam.

So, in all, perhaps He would countenance
Heimweh for a madhouse, humanly speaking
Prefer Rhoda the hippopotamus whose daughter's a bitch,
Jack-o'-the Blade who is handy at his wrists,
And something tells me all those motes,
Collective maculae, might make a beam
That would sustain a sane world, my masters,
And utilise Spandau for peevish purposes.

Who'd be sent there, and by whom, is matter for another poem.

A Paella for Drivellers

'And Swift expires a Driv'ler and a Show'.
—Samuel Johnson: *The Vanity of Human Wishes*

i.

Translated from Mater of Misericordia
To Pater of *saeva indignatio*
That way the classical finks like Bobbie Graves
can't get at you: though I could
beat most of them at their olives and *ludus*)
Is best perhaps a time to take stocks:
Verbena annoys me: what does it smell like?
Also the gladioli the two Marys brought me
And were flushed by some prunish sister
Or some old segotia over-doing his duty.
(In Mercers a dear old thing
grieved the absence of brandies
and nice things on the Christmas board,
she'd had a Guinness or two, God help her.)

'Beauty is difficult', Yeats told the
Pigeon, and Pound quoted him from
His Pisan cage. The old muddled
Eagle snarled at Paquin. O what
An imprisonment was his: not even
Old Graves could let his portrait
Rest in peace in the White House in Limerick.
Ugliness is difficult. Claudius Graves
Achieved it. My curse on the sage.
May his translations from Suetonius to Apuleius
Prove inaccurate: his novels be

Pulped for faeces-paper:
The *Tonton Macoutes* be his *Legio Mariae*:
His White Goddess be proven a personal deity of Perón:
His fame be enshrined in the theology of Father O'Flynn
Or Maeterlinck the guest of Salazar.
Let him be honoured by the Caudillo,
Haunted by the shades of Allende and Neruda,
May the shade of La Passionaria
Vomit the blood of the innocent
On his perfidious Anglo-Irish ashes:
Albion's paltry gain is Ireland's
Unspeakably sales-bargain loss. We
Salute Tom Moore, the friend of
Emmet and Byron: he never
Sold his soul for a pottage
Of peevery against giants.
Bobbie's last ride with Laura made him no Petrarch.
I hate him. Hatred is good
When it is for the senile monomaniac,
For the lowest type of Irishman,
The begrudger. Yes, he is a good poet.
P.G. Wodehouse was a good jester.
William Joyce was a good newscaster.
They had not the time to strip
Yeats and Joyce and Eliot and
Poor great Ezra whose Cantos are
Our glory, our blotched, marvellous, glory.
Our Europe, mullioned, impounded
In choate tiles of splendour.

ii.

But I wander as usual.
I could never be Leander.
For my heroes are people I fear to fight for:
Jews, Sephardic and Ashkenazy,
Palestine refugees, disloyal Kurds,
The world's great galaxy of Nansens,
God's chosen miserable. The
Most I would or might do would
Be defend a queer or take
Umbrage against 'nigger'-haters.

iii.

O Lord, why are we so afraid.
We should not need miracles.
Moses and Aaron did their thing in their time.
So did Jesus. But they were
Superstars setting precedents which
Were not guaranteed for eternal charts:
Planets have been violated (I
Suppose, of course, Jesus violated Earth)
And yet we are afraid of things
Less mundane than miracles:
Afraid of our neighbour's goodwill,
Afraid of our enemies' plámás,
Afraid of our priests, our public servants,
Afraid of the Jones's car,
Afraid of ourselves and the Unknown Gods
While saintly Bobbie lives,
Scandalizes the good people of Limerick,
For which he professed himself homesick.

iv.

Yes: Eavan Boland, poet and daughter of Elizabeth's Chancellor,
Was right. I am mentally sick:
Sick of verbena and gladioli and Graves.
My place is St. Elizabeth's.
Not this Swiftian haven where even the mad are human
And the Unknown God turds a globule of grace.
Lord, I am grateful even for being afraid,
And I remember you, Faith Burton,
Who thought you were a tram,
And you, dear Covington, who were bled by faggotry,
        Gésinus and leukaemia,
And Anton of the grimed ivory neck,
Mason who Candied up with Terry,
Whisky in Vaucresson, Pernod
When the movie-director's wife,
Stuffed with baby, stuffed me with
Francs in the Bar Vert.
Above all, Lord, Unknown God,
I am grateful for finding
My choate tiles of splendour
In poor human beasts,
Not in *putti* or medallions.
These human things are all we have.
God, Unknown or *à la* Nine Fridays
Be good to them. God bless *le moineau*
And make her a good girl:
Rich and rare were the gems she wore.
Now we are rid of our greatest carbuncle.

Austin, though you are cinders,
Thou should'st be with us now.

Abbey Press Lunch: 3/9/69

for Phil O'Kelly

Airy from early communion with Austin's monks,
Liberty Hall around the corner, I twiddle
Glass of lemony non-sin, dare not fiddle
Proscript of Antrim doctor, forbidden
Alcohol. I talk to Eamon.
Keen on priorities, he dared a Minister,
Daemon-struck, was suspended, let back in.
Long ago for a Larkin under Toto
We mummed together at Olympia.
Now we burble about ancients and Sophocles
In the Kingdom: Mac, great auk in wild earth.
I talk to Alan: not today nor yesterday
We had pillow talk with Hilton:
'Two angels at my bedside!'
Low at High Table, far from Everest's brother,
I am astonished to recall I
Lugged Laffan across *The Shadowy Waters:* he
Tells of Patrick-Tarry, Scotched in the stalls
Approached by Earnán: 'Do you remember me?'
'Indeed I do'. Blith on a hustings
Corner-boys cornered him. 'Three boos
For Blythe who never blessed himself'.
I looked down the table: Senior Critics
Serenade Hunt. But where is Gaby?
Has Fallon fallen by the wayside?
And Ó Faracháin. Has he foreseen
Fíon that without doubt is not *Gan Mhoirt*?
(At least my sip). I am happy.

Why do critics bore me, academics awe me
Editors chill me, alone poets and mummers
Throw up a Maginot Front (and we all know what came of that)
Against our common humanity. Huns, Vandals, all
Bent on spoliating the rose,
Redesigning the heart, converting
Tender feelings to colly-wobbles.
And of course even among the poets and mummers
There are Eichmanns and Quislings and types
Who'd be quite happy to be Ministers of Hate,
Or speculate with non-conservationists,

Or curse our beloved clergy,
Or even take a turn at harassing Hilary Boyle.
—But meandering mind damned
By something said by Vincent D.
I navigate the table and feel fond
Of Finegan, Seamus, Gus and Rushe,
Hunt's starry fays who cluster round their allocated prey
And do their job while I play with mummers.

In conclusion, Phil, while thanking you for lunch,
I've a strong hunch some of the mummers I name-drop
Will come to my funeral. Indeed
You're welcome yourself if you get a comp.
After this mild romp, outside again
To my wonderful city, and the Liffey
Seems to smell of greasepaint,
And clouds are balls of cleansing tissue
And the buses are a toccata of Galuppi
And lamp-posts reach to the dressing-room
Of stars that, piteously, will survive my poor frail mummers.

Postscript to Patrician Stations

for Richard Riordan

No more
Like a rat in a corner.
No more
Like a bat in a trap
But luminous, humble, triumphant
I accept defeat. I know body and soul
At the feet of trencher-men, trust to the last
In honour, the solemn word, the judicious nod,
O what a sell if body and soul have gone to Pilates.
No matter   I am still
No more
Like a rat in a corner.

[Dublin, 1969]

Contra Naturam

i.

I am hopeless about
Trees, shrubs, flowers:
Though I suppose
I'd parley with a dandelion or daisy
If my nose were trained
To flair nature:
A rose at a pinch.

In the main
I detest God's very own country
Wild, seed-packeted or parterred.
In my secret walks
I gibber like a loon
Against the Maker:
The wizard of waterfalls
The custodian of cataracts
The major-domo of mountains
The inventor of oaks
The generalissimo of the garden-pea.

And that goes too for
Luna clustered round with all
Her starry what-d'ya-callums,
Bee-loud glades, airy glens,
The Seven Bens, Everest, Etna:
All 'tourist attractions'
Designed to distract from the main issue:
Our insensate captivity
Our banishment from Eden.

ii.

Confession, self-analysis,
Vanity of vanities.
The air this morning
Was veined with ice.
The sky this morning
Had taken the blue-bag.
The light this morning
Was braying like a Sitwell.
I sloshed through a goulash,
Wet brown leafage.
A brat of a dog
Leaped at me.
The beast was friendly.
A brace of copper beeches
Easy to recognise, and he
Might win me round.

[Dublin, 1970]

Second Thoughts

Ascending descending
in the ethereal verbena
swallows dip wings
to jazzed-up *paseo*
light, light guerdon

kisses o kisses peach
the stone ochre stone
of the Church of San Pedro.
In the Holy City of Avila.

Coruscating syncopating
ebonite blackness
factitious stars emerald
ruby grenadine
mantillas in apple
waterfalls in silver
pluming smoke palm-trees
odour of cordite.
In the Holy City of Avila.

O what a squall
sent the Sierra
chair hooked table
glass ticked off bottle
little ones ululated
old ones castigated
flight of the innocents
denser the plumage of
'The Eagle of Gredos'
In the Holy City of Avila.

And I curse the turgid
René Füllop-Miller
easier not to know
plundered New World gold
paid the last builders' bills
for the Convent of San José.
Did Teresa ever give a damn
for the discalced Indian?
In the Holy City of Avila.

[Avila, July 1971]

Who Walks Through Salamanca

for Pearse Hutchinson

Who walks through Salamanca
in air of bronze weightless,
forgotten, no, absolved,
the long chains of anguish
slush of three o'clock
in the etiolated mornings
merited pangs
inflicted by the meritless
exploded gladioli
diamonds cutting the panes of the heart.

Who walks through Salamanca
by platinum dreams bespangled,
apprehended, no, encompassed,
the staccati of turpitude
chill of three o'clock
in the horn-torn mornings
gratuitous goring
bulldazed by the goggled
strumpeted lilies
excremental squatting of the soul.

Who dreams in Salamanca
of the flowering body
and the fecund mind
and forgets the rest of Juvenal
the faggotry the screeching
the insatiable women,
phoenixed in bland acceptance

of 'the tragic sense of life'.
Send us Unamuño both
children of Janus
your aureoled peppery benedictions.

[Salamanca, August 1971]

On First Hearing of the Death of W.H. Auden

Peach, tangerine,
the clouds, the mortals,
and the bus
toward Ròdos.

All the glitter of cats
ignorant of passing
departing shrouds.

The mewling icons are playing *veroñicas*
the prepuced minarets are weeping
and the conserved hinds and does
and all manner of things
shed ironic mourning.

So do the copper-haired Graces,
the single *Suzuki* decked with carnations,
the nits in the public places
and my sprig of caraway from the mosque.

Layabout strangers
limestone specialists
lingering serenaders
lament an exodus.

Myrtles are not in fashion.
I am tormented by ignorance of the names of flowers.

I pick up my match-box.
I read, 'Wistaria'.
'Wistaria', Wystan, wanhope, Wien.

Limestone into limestone.

[Ròdos, 2-3 October 1973]

After the 'Sentences' of A.C.

They talk of peace with justice
Parade their Rosary ways
But we remember how they tortured
Stephen Hayes.

[Dublin, 28 December 1974]

Pastiche

'Thomas McGreevy
Heard unearthly music
Passing westward
Over Stephen's Green'.

When was that written?
What year of the salads?
With whom did I share the crystal?
How long after the poor bitch Europe
Ceased to quiver?

I think it was forty-eight
A year of premature resurrection
A year of dung and primroses;
The man in Portugal will tell you.

But we all forget so much:
Crystal, primroses, dung.
That man who announced his parity of spirit,
His intention to read all Shaw,
Then ascend into Heaven.
The patience of Job cannot make us Marcels.

The unearthly music has passed by.

[Dublin, 19-20 February 1975]

Staff Nurse

She is above bed-pans.
The bawls of trapped buttocks
For attention do not move her.
If in eternity of aluminium vice
Muscle shifted and hope was lost
In the bed of excrement,
The ice of her scorn
Would frigidare the Bold Fenian Men,
For she is cold as the Hell of the Gael.

She never heard a nightingale,
Might fancy herself as Cavell at dawn;
Yet would put the fear of God
In that Albanian nun who rescues little ones
From garbage; in my dreams
She is Irma the Terrible.
O lady, you are harsh,
I pray you be not harsher when
Raised to the Sisterhood.

[Dublin, 1976]

For Julius Henry Marx (1891-1977)

Among the blazing azaleas
Of the Parque del Campo Grande
I perceived the true, sophisticated
Marxist point of view:
Let the people have duck soup;
Let them at the races lose their shirts,
Let them shirtless storm the Opera,
And stop the shrieks of Mimi with Coronas.
Chiefly, let them raise intemperate eyebrows
To the infinite spaces of the stars.

[Vallodolid-Madrid, 12 August-1 September 1977]

During the Illness of Dolores Ibarruri

The honourable old woman returns
Treasured by all: even brown.
The forty years have been worth it,
But the cracked heart knows its frown.

Not alone Spain's spirit
But of all who care
For dignity, love, comradeship,
For minutes night rare.

And I think of Kathleen Daly Clarke
Whom we exported to English welfare,
And her spouse the tobacconist.

[Madrid, September 1977]

Without Her Cloak

The last time we met
(Mild May before the year you plunged into strong waters)
You said: 'They were very good to me'.
So in walled Avila of unspeakable Teresa
I recalled you to the manager of the Hotel Jardín.
It was the Feast of the Assumption.

A useful cliché that same high Castilian courtesy.
Fortuitously, of course, the argent is real.
When I told him you were dead
        (Dead, though you walk beside
         me, cloaked, ribald, vulnerable)
His dark mild eyes crinkled.
The argent real was in his threnody:
La pobre Mees Katie—twice.

[Valladolid, August 1977]

Piedad

I am lame at the bar in Atocha.
'Your knee is wounded, she says.
I press a coin in her copper palm.
She gives me a prayer for graces
From the Christ: composed by a foreigner,
Gemma Galgani.
Lord, am I in eternal Spain
Or Italianate Ireland of the craven hussies.

[Valladolid, 21 August 1977]

To Ms Mae West on Her 85th

What right have you?
Did you pat your platinum alps
When across the electric wire
The thrilling message came
That the pelvic muscles were tranquillized
The gluteal shivers forever fridged
That in fact (O lamentable extinction!)
Elvis had gone pop.

Or did you cable another Cadillac
To some lucky mother-doll of Christ's
Or over caskets run your pensive eye,
Golden, placid, lined with peachy silk,
And have your self re-measured
For the last tango with the beautician
Who'll set all curves in proper mould,
The plastic dugs on top?

I weep not for the 'King': he wasn't my type.
(Well, give him some pink, false roses.)
But you, old-timer, had better go West
While the pickings (pan me a nugget, Beulah)
Are ripe. The blue jeans of yesteryear
Might yet reverence your mummy,
And e'en their grassed spawn be mesmerized.

[Vallodolid, 17 August 1977]

The Last Romantic

I see with love the turbaned skull
The flower hand beckoning to bosky doom.
I see with love the purblind balls
Tracing *Madame Bovary* in an ill-lit room.

[Madrid, September 1977]

Málaga

'Es un loco?'—was my roar,
When the nutty Andaluz awoke me,
Prodded, scratched, sibilant for cigarettes.
'Un poco mas o menos', yawned the whore.
'A little more or less'.
And then no more, while the tawny beast
From the heavens consumed me.

That night the monkey
Peddled me grass from the port,
Fresh weed of Africa,
But I cast my bread on coarse gin,
Slugged in the ebony and spume of dawn.

[Málaga, August 1978]

Micheál

25 October 1899—6 March 1978

Doffed the curious toupées
Unflaked the valorous *maquillage*

—A pale olive haze
On special days
As when Lennox
Going to the ball
Plastered his face green
For no reason at all—

The great player relaxes
(Does he smoke a Celtique?)
Waits for this ultimate call.
'O what will people say?'

In a sub-tropical garden
Drenched in moonlight
Moths, midges, white butterflies,
Die on my cheeks
As I cry for you.

[Málaga, August 1978]

Lolek [1]

Czestochowa, Jasna Gora, Auschwitz, Nova Huta:
Archdiocesan Cracow:

Symphony of ashed flesh and steel and Mary,
Uncountable dark nights in the factory of death,
Salvos of laud on the Black Virgin's White Mountain,
The people of God keen from metal with metamorphosed hearts
Expectancy and rose of Christ's fair state
You have known it all:
Grease-paint, desk, sledge-hammer,
Arc-light, explosive, grammar,
Mickiewicz's mighty line
More resounding than Wagnerian microphones,
Juliusz Slowacki in the Szkackas' drawingroom,
Promethean Cyprian Norwid,
Poor Zegladlowicz who pained the clergy
And Juan de la Cruz wrestling,
Parched in a tawny landscape,
With the Angel of Faith.

You expect much faith from Patrick's children.
In this our pleasant land of Country and Western singers,
So great a hope as yours must find it.
And meantime—while the phones ring and the keys tap
          and the words spawn—
Let the chisellers and the unstained
Sing a carol for Karol:
'May Holy Ireland be holier,
Perhaps even made whole'.

[Feast of the Assumption, Dublin 1979]

[1] Boyhood diminutive of 'Karol' Wojtyla, Pope John Paul 2nd

Flying Men

'Come fly to me'
Was his Master's voice,
And Joseph of Copertino zoomed.
'Come fly with me'
Was his own hortation,
And he seized the Confessor of
The Convent of Fossombrone,
Took him, men, on a trip.

But O the Chevalier Baldassare
Who had fierce, O such fierce, tremors!
At Assisi they say it happened.
Joseph grabbed him by the hair
Wheeled him round in aether
And from the brightness of the air
Set him down safe, O untrembling.

We Irish are not to be outdone
We have our very own flying man:
No monk, I grant you, but almost as good,
He was cursed by one.

His name was Suibhne.

[Dublin, May 25, 1979]

The Poetic Touch

A dachshund races a lawnmower.
There are John West salmon roses
And cream. A deserted plastic swan
Keels in the parched grass. These things,
I reckon, our rostrum explicators
Would bid us dwell upon.

I cannot make it new.
Light glints in crevices of cloud:
Enough to be doing with.

[Churchtown, June 1979]

St. Pius Ward

for Brendan Harding

Stately, scrawny, hot-eyed, head alert
To some unearthly music, and O steered
By twin snowy handmaidens, he proceeds
In majesty: plucking at some
Kind of embroidery frame, flexed
Frightfully to a flask of bluey wine.

I dread his return. Apocalypse! Cover
Mine eyes. His face dazzles. I live again
The blood-gush of a Catalan Christmas,
Root at the walnuts of a Cardinal's brain.

Christ, that my death were in my arms!

[Galway, August 1982]

Peacock and Little Bull

for Helen and Ursula

From Doohat to Annaghmakerrig
I slosh through *café-au-lait* pools
Squelch through burnt amber leafage
Slag branches where the wind misrules
And cogitate that uncommon fowl
Laid up for how long, O Juno?

How long may that delirium of jewels
Share darkness with rats, straw, calf?
How long will that pomp, that plenitude
Sustain lustre, glitter, sheen,
Against reversion to the brighter scene?

Our peacock, no doubt, mocks our alien ruth
Perceives for fantasy our callow truth:
His ivory tower that manacled shed
His constant worshipper that small bull's head.

The Short Unhappy Exile of Don Geraldo

14th May—21 June 1984

(para mi amigo, John Liddy, gran
aficionado de las cantinas, como yo)

I wished to die, but yes, I wished to die,
till they said I'd drive them mad,
but not in a clean and well-lit place,
exiled from my things,
from my black tobacco,
from my roses,
from the street
Carlos Gross had them name for me,
poor Carlos whom I've survived.

Quiero morirme
here in Alhaurin el Grande
babbling, they'd have me believe,
of my dear glamorous shades,
of Lytton and Ralph and Carrington,
of Leonard, Virginia and Morgan.
Yes, I wish to die.

Only let me connect,
dreaming, dreaming, dreaming,
till they raise the coverlet
beyond my nostrils.

NOTES

Second Letter: To Patrick Swift, p. 47
Patrick Swift (1928-83), the artist, who was a friend of John Jordan since their school-days.

The Chime, p.63
B.G. Achong, the celebrated medical scientist, and friend at Oxford University.

Fourth Letter to David Posner, p.68
David Louis Posner (1923-57), the American poet and a friend at Oxford University.

'Entre Chat Et Loup', p. 71
Quentin Stevenson (b. 1935), the English poet and a friend at Oxford University.

The Feast of St. Justin, p.95
Frank Ryan and Stephen Hayes, two IRA leaders from the 1940s. See also the poem 'After the Sentences of A.C.' (Austin Clarke).

Letter to Paul, p. 97
Paul Durcan, the poet.

During the illness of Dolores Ibarruri, p. 124
La Pasionaria, the iconic Spanish Republican leader.

Without Her Cloak, p.125
La pobre Mees Katie: Kate O'Brien, the novelist, a close friend.

Micheál, p.130
Micheál Mac Liammóir, the celebrated actor, and friend at the Gate Theatre.

The Short Unhappy Exile of Don Geraldo, p. 136
Gerald Brenan (1894-1987), the Hispanophile writer of Irish descent best known for *The Spanish Labyrinth,* an historical work on the background to the Spanish Civil War, and for *South From Granada: Seven Years in an Andalusian Village.*

Printed in the United Kingdom
by Lightning Source UK Ltd.
127197UK00001B/595-630/A